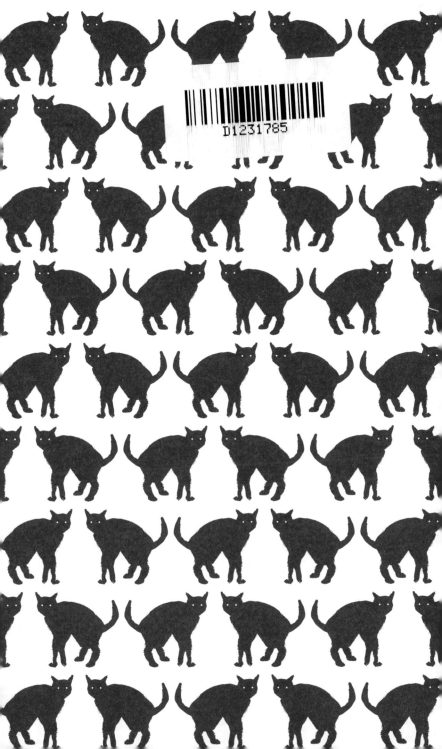

D1231785

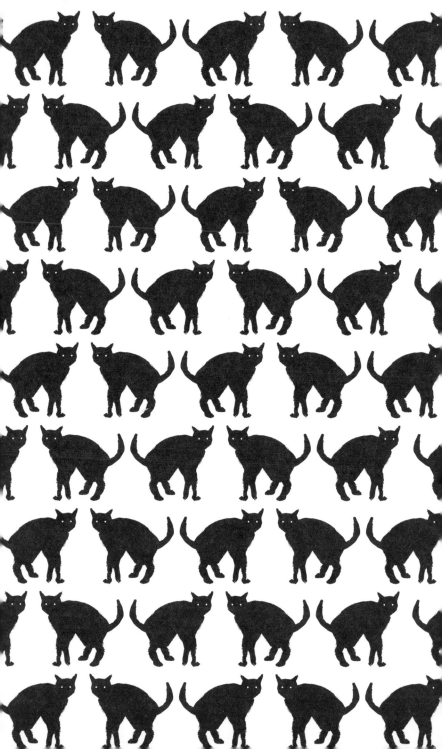

SCOTTISH
CATS

Hamish Whyte, poet, editor and publisher, was born in Renfrewshire and educated in Glasgow, where he lived and worked as a librarian for many years. He moved to Edinburgh in 2004. He has published several collections of poetry, edited many anthologies of Scottish literature and runs Mariscat Press, which has published collections by poets such as Edwin Morgan and Douglas Dunn. He is an Honorary Research Fellow in the Department of Scottish Literature, Glasgow University. In his spare time he plays percussion with Edinburgh band The Whole Shebang.

Scottish
Cats

An Anthology of Poems

EDITED BY
Hamish Whyte

BIRLINN

First published in 2013 by
Birlinn Limited
West Newington House
10 Newington Road, Edinburgh
EH9 1QS

www.birlinn.co.uk

ISBN-13: 978 1 78027 139 2

British Library Cataloguing-in-Publication Data
A catalogue record for this book is available from the British
Library

Designed and illustrated by James Hutcheson
Set in Monotype Poliphilus and Blado

Printed and bound by
Proost NV, Belgium

CONTENTS

*To Anne Harrison, who loves cats and
Lizzie MacGregor, who loves anthologies.*

INTRODUCTION

'An excellent companion for
A literary gentleman, a cat',
Said fat auld Gautier,
And, Dod, he was richt, at that.
SYDNEY GOODSIR SMITH

CATS HAVE ALWAYS HAD A SPECIAL APPEAL TO POETS, perhaps because they seem to exhibit so many human traits, not least that characteristic Scottish attribute, thrawnness. And Britain's only indigenous cat, the Scottish wildcat, is held up to Scots as an example of fierce independence. (It has also by its agility added to the language in the phrase *tummle one's wilkies* – tumble head over heels – from *tummel the wulcat.*)

According to legend the Scots were the first northern people to keep cats – Fergus I of Scotland (fl.330 BC) is said to have brought them from Portugal, his ancestors having taken cats there from Egypt – but judging by the many stories of cruelty towards cats, Scots have not been especially kind to them. Witness the charming pastime of 'cat in the barrel', in which a cat was hung up in a small barrel half-filled with soot and, in Bishop Percy's words, 'a parcel of clowns on horseback tried to beat out the ends of it, in order to show their dexterity in escaping before the contents fell upon them.' Worse, if it can be believed, was the ceremony of the Taighheirm, which supposedly took place in the Western Isles until the seventeenth century. In this ghastly rite black cats were roasted alive to summon spirits from Hell and reward the sacrificer with riches and second sight. From the evidence of the Scottish witch trials the cat would appear to have been a common sacrificial animal, often baptized before being killed. Two hundred years later Neil Munro as a boy received a present of a catapult with a note attached: 'From an uncle who does not like cats.'

The record is not all bad. Cats which have always been tolerated, if not loved, are those valued for their usefulness, like Towser the famous mouser of Glenturret Distillery (who in his 23-year-old life accounted for 27,000 mice) and the Glasgow People's Palace cat Smudge who was a paid-up member of the GMBATU. The list of Scottish literary ailurophiles is long enough: Walter Scott, Byron, Thomas Carlyle, Joanna Baillie, Andrew Lang, Willa Muir, Compton Mackenzie, Sydney Goodsir Smith, George MacBeth et al. And a goodly number of Scottish poets particularly seem to have taken cats to their hearts.

The poems in *Scottish Cats* explore the poets' feline relationships, from Henryson's fifteenth-century account of 'Gib Hunter, Our Jolie Cat', through eighteenth-century Aesopian fables, nineteenth-century cat and mouse tussles, to contemporary musings on this domestic but mysterious animal – 'tame but not *tamed*', 'the tiger who eats from the hand', as the Japanese saying is: many of the poets exploit this ambivalence (see especially Alastair Reid's 'Propinquity'). And there is a preoccupation with a perceived correlation between cats and poems. There is also, as Gautier wrote in his introduction to Baudelaire's *Fleurs du Mal*, a nocturnal side to cats, strange and cabalistic, which is very seductive to the poet. This aspect is perhaps hinted at in Joseph Macleod's strange 'A Strange Cat Got In' or 'Cat‑Faith' by Alastair Reid. The poems are certainly not all serious: there are Edwin Morgan's verbally playful cats, for example, and Jackie Kay's 'The Nine Lives of the Cat Mandu', into which she tries to cram as many cat puns and proverbs as she can – cats have always been a good source of wise saws ('Well kens the Mouse that the Cat's out of the House').

I have also included a clutch of nursery rhymes. Compton Mackenzie in his *Cats' Company* wrote 'In the Nursery Rhymes, the cat always has precedence' and there are at least a dozen traditional Scottish cat rhymes and several more literary ones. 'Pussy‑cat, Pussy‑cat' is probably one of the best known of all nursery rhymes; the Scottish version ('Poussie, poussie baudrons') first appeared in print in Robert Chambers's *The Popular Rhymes of Scotland*, 1842. The version included here is from the 1870 edition. Baudrons, by the way, is the familiar Scots name for cat. I should confess also that I have shamelessly raided my earlier anthology, *The Scottish Cat*.

The poems of course do not aim to discover any elemental Scottishness in our cats – as noted, the only truly Scottish cat is the wildcat – but it is a truism that when we write about animals we are writing about ourselves. Scottish poets evidently subscribe to Christopher Smart's opinion of his cat: 'he is good to think on, if a man would express himself neatly.'

HAMISH WHYTE

Cat and Mous

Said the poussie
Til the mousie,
'Let me intil
Your wee housie.
We will play
And we will sing
And we will dance
A jingo-ring.'

Said the mousie
Til the poussie,
'Ye'll no get
In my wee housie.
Ye are big
And I am wee
And ye wad eat me
For your tea.'

J.K. Annand (1908-1993)

The Kitten

Wanton droll, whose harmless play
Beguiles the rustic's closing day,
When, drawn the evening fire about,
Sit aged crone and thoughtless lout,
And child upon his three-foot stool,
Waiting until his supper cool,
And maid, whose cheek outblooms the rose,
As bright the blazing fagot glows,
Who, bending to the friendly light,
Plies her task with busy sleight;
Come, show thy tricks and sportive graces,
Thus circled round with merry faces!

  Backward coil'd and crouching low,
With glaring eyeballs watch thy foe,
The housewife's spindle whirling round,
Or thread, or straw that on the ground
Its shadow throws, by urchin sly
Held out to lure thy roving eye;
The stealing onward, fiercely spring
Upon the tempting faithless thing.
Now, wheeling round with bootless skill,
Thy bo-peep tail provokes thee still,
As still beyond thy curving side
Its jetty tip is seen to glide;

Till from thy centre starting far,
Thou sidelong veerst with rump in air
Erected stiff, and gait awry,
Like madam in her tantrums high;
Though ne'er a madam of them all,
Whose silken kirtle sweeps the hall,
More varied trick and whim displays
To catch the admiring stranger's gaze.

Doth power in measured verses dwell,
All thy vagaries wild to tell
Ah no! the start, the jet, the bound,
The giddy scamper round and round,
With leap and toss and high curvet,
And many a whirling somerset,
(Permitted by the modern muse
Expression technical to use)
These mock the deftest rhymester's skill,
But poor in art, though rich in will.

The featest tumbler, stage bedight,
To thee is but a clumsy wight,
Who every limb and sinew strains
To do what costs thee little pains;
For which, I trow, the gaping crowd
Requite him oft with plaudits loud.

But, stopp'd the while thy wanton play,
Applauses too thy pains repay;
For then, beneath some urchin's hand
With modest pride thou tak'st thy stand,
While many a stroke of kindness glides
Along thy back and tabby sides.
Dilated swells thy glossy fur,
And loudly croons thy busy purr,
As, timing well the equal sound,
Thy clutching feet bepat the ground,
And all their harmless claws disclose
Like prickles of an early rose,
While softly from thy whisker'd cheek
Thy half-closed eyes peer, mild and meek.

But not alone by cottage fire
Do rustics rude thy feats admire.
The learned sage, whose thoughts explore
The widest range of human lore,
Or with unfetter'd fancy fly
Through airy heights of poesy,
Pausing smiles with alter'd air
To see thee climb his elbow-chair,
Or, struggling on the mat below,
Hold warfare with his slipper'd toe.
The widow'd dame or lonely maid,
Who, in the still but cheerless shade
Of home unsocial, spends her age,

And rarely turns a letter'd page,
Upon her hearth for thee lets fall
The rounded cork or paper ball,
Nor chides thee on thy wicked watch,
The ends of ravell'd skein to catch,
But lets thee have thy wayward will,
Perplexing oft her better skill.

E'en he, whose mind of gloomy bent,
In lonely tower or prison pent,
Reviews the coil of former days,
And loathes the world and all its ways,
What time the lamp's unsteady gleam
Hath roused him from his moody dream,
Feels, as thou gambol'st round his seat,
His heart of pride less fiercely beat,
And smiles, a link in thee to find,
That joins it still to living kind.

Whence hast thou then, thou witless puss!
The magic power to charm us thus?
Is it that in thy glaring eye
And rapid movements, we descry –
Whilst we at ease, secure from ill,
The chimney corner snugly fill –
A lion darting on his prey,
A tiger at his ruthless play?

Or is it that in thee we trace,
With all thy varied wanton grace,
An emblem, view'd with kindred eye,
Of tricky, restless infancy?
Ah! many a lightly sportive child,
Who hath like thee our wits beguiled,
To dull and sober manhood grown,
With strange recoil our hearts disown.

And so, poor kit! must thou endure,
When thou becom'st a cat demure,
Full many a cuff and angry word,
Chased roughly from the tempting board.
But yet, for that thou hast, I ween,
So oft our favour'd play-mate been,
Soft be the change which thou shalt prove!
When time hath spoil'd thee of our love,
Still be thou deem'd by housewife fat
A comely, careful, mousing cat,
Whose dish is, for the public good,
Replenish'd oft with savoury food,
Nor, when thy span of life is past,
Be thou to pond or dung-hill cast,
But, gently borne on goodman's spade,
Beneath the decent sod be laid,
And children show with glistening eyes
The place where poor old pussy lies.

Joanna Baillie (1762-1851)

The Cat and the Man

I

The old cat sat by the fire,
And never stirred;
She had lapped her allowance of milk,
Had washed, and purred.

And now she sat, eyes closed,
A feline sphinx,
Taking a cat's equivalent
For forty winks.

* * * * *

An ear uprose,
And a quick glance stole
To the back of the hearth
Where was what seemed a hole.

But she did not move;
Just quietly sat —
Years had made that
The gift of the cat.

Cold she seemed still,
But an inward fire
Burned in that veiled glance,
And flamed desire.

The raised ear sank;
Calm head never swerved,
Only the fore claws
Clutchingly curved;

And then uncurved,
As the cat uprose
Arched her back,
Stretched out her toes;

And she sank back
Quiet in soul,
But giving a casual
Glance at the hole.

2

It stares at the fire,
That gleams back from its eyes,
And no man can fathom
What in them lies.

Seeing, unseeing,
Their steadfast gaze,
What can it discern
In the heart of the blaze?

Does the cat when it takes
Its forty winks
Go back in truth
To the days of the Sphinx?

Unchangeable he
Since the days of old,
Sitting there motionless,
Placid, cold;

Content to sit
Till the crack of doom,
Wild cat of the woods,
Tame cat in a room.

For afield or in wood,
In hut or in house,
They have watched for ages
For bird or mouse.

And time is nothing,
They wait and wait,
Till comes the hour
And the stroke of fate.

And so sits the cat,
Ever the same,
Hunter implacable,
Wild or tame;

Takes his ironical
Forty winks,
Packed with red fury
Still as the Sphinx;

Despising the dog's
Subservient clan
As the aristocrat
Looks upon man;

Casual comes
And casual goes,
Finical down to
The tips of his toes;

Strolls abroad
And takes the air
And surveys the world
As if quite detached
From anything there . . .

Robert Bain (1865–1955)

Baudron's Sang

The gudewife birrs wi the wheel a day,
Three threeds an a thrum,
Three threeds an a thrum,
A walth o wark an sma time for play,
Wi the lint sae white and worset grey,
Work hard she maun, while sing I may –
Three threeds an a thrum,
Three threeds an a thrum.

The gudewife rises out o her bed,
Three threeds an a thrum,
Three threeds an a thrum,
Wi her cozy nicht-mutch around her head,
To steer the fire to a blaze sae red,
Her feet I rub wi welcome glad,
Three threeds an a thrum,
Three threeds an a thrum.

I dander round her wi blythsome birr,
Three threeds an a thrum,
Three threeds an a thrum,
An rub on her legs my sleek warm fur,
Wi sweeps o my tail I welcome her,
An round her rin wherever she stir,
Three threeds an a thrum,
Three threeds an a thrum.

The men folks' time for rest is gie sma —
Three threeds an a thrum,
Three threeds an a thrum,
They're out in sunshine, an out in snaw;
Tho cauld winds whistle, or rain should fa,
I, i the ingle, do nought ava;
Three threeds an a thrum,
Three threeds an a thrum.

I like the gudeman, but loe the wife,
Three threeds an a thrum,
Three threeds an a thrum,
Days mony they've seen o toil, an strife,
O sorrow the human hours are rife,
Their hands been mine a the days o my life,
Three threeds an a thrum,
Three threeds an a thrum.

Auld baudrons grey, she kittened me here,
Three threeds an a thrum,
Three threeds an a thrum,
An wha was my sire, I ne'er did speir;
Brithers and sisters smoored i the weir,
Left me alane to my mither dear,
Three threeds an a thrum,
Three threeds an a thrum.

An syne she loed me muckle mair,
Three threeds an a thrum,
Three threeds an a thrum,
For want o her weans near a taen frae'r
Her only kitten she couldna spare,
I a healing was to her heart sae sair,
Three threeds an a thrum,
Three threeds an a thrum.

As I grew a cat, wi look sae douce,
Three threeds an a thrum,
Three threeds an a thrum,
She learnt me to catch the pilfrin moose,
Wi the thief-like rottens I had nae truce,
But banished them frae the maister's hoose,
Three threeds an a thrum,
Three threeds an a thrum.

Mither got fushionless, auld an blin,
Three threeds an a thrum,
Three threeds an a thrum,
The bluid in her veins was cauld an thin,
Her claws were blunt an she couldna rin,
An tae her forebears she was gathered in,
Three threeds an a thrum,
Three threeds an a thrum.

Now I sit hurklin aye i the ase,
Three threeds an a thrum,
Three threeds an a thrum,
The queen I am o that cosy place;
As wi ilka paw I dicht my face,
I sing an purr wi mickle grace,
Three threeds an a thrum,
Three threeds an a thrum

[anon.]

Poetry Circle in a Square Room

In the centre of the room
a squat man in a bulgy suit
has put his cap under the chair
upside down into which he coils
a snake like a scarf.
He knows it is not a snake.

It might be convenient if it were
for his nostrils sense the
woman enter, seat herself behind
in the far corner. As she crosses
her legs under the red silk
dressing gown there is the
silk worm sound in his ear.

She contemplates the grey,
horn-rimmed girl with the flat
shoes (perhaps she can write)
sitting on the outermost edge,
angular in the front row.
She opens a new note-book.

Snow falls. Snow falls.
A black cat is at the window.
The lecturer will not let
the poem in, dismisses
its green eyes to the darkness.
The black cat leaps from the snow,
stares at the pane,
silent, asserting nothing:
leap – a felt movement,

effortlessly creating the
moment that is one thing,
her poise, less precarious,
she acknowledges, perhaps,
our world inside. The snow,
a blank page, acknowledges
her delicate tread, her imprint
of a moon-lit traverse.

Precise shadow, you are
a presence to be shut out.
Admitted, your intolerable
completeness would destroy us.

George Bruce (1909–2002)

Tale of a Cat

I didn't want her at first, not liking cats,
Takers of the birds that in hundreds in the spring set the woods
Astir with song, set the branches uttering green;
But one night in March when I opened the door of the kitchen
To stars and the beech hedge rattling with last year's leaves,
There she shivered in the track of light
Springing across the grass.

She fled into dark when I went out to fetch or to chase her;
I wasn't sure which.
Next day the cat-loving neighbours out on this hilltop
Were dropping their hints about kindness of cat-keeping;
I scowled from my catless paradise.

Next, though, she was curled near my step
In the March sunlight;
When I went outside she was rubbing herself on my ankle,
Tottered on weak legs,
Spine like string-pearls under my hand,
Tail thin as a rat's tail, and she leaf-frail, leaf-tremulous,
Atom
Under the sky;
I grunted, and opened a tin of sardines,
The spines infolded like silvery chains.

And so that began it. I tried to adapt to the new
        charge,
Though now and again, nights after, fantasised that
I took her out under the unclouded moon
(Her head bobbing in my arms as she wondered where
        she was going)
Set her in the centre of a field
As Hansel and Gretel once were set in the dark forest,
And ran away, and left her.

I didn't want this life.
I didn't want this life.
But back she would come, scratching at the door, as a
        steel nib scratches a page,
Wanting only to be taken in and kept,
Saying, if not in words, I am life, I am life, accept,
        accept.
Fierce-fanged, curve-clawed, rasp-tongued happy life.

I woke, as from a long limbo.
So the tins of catfood I bought from the shop were an
        anchor of sorts,
Stopped me from drifting away in my sterile sublime.

Now
She has me, the strawberry blonde
Who crosses her nose with her paws if I try to kiss it,
Or sits, sometimes, a Buddha, on the couch,

Paws neatly folded below,
Suffering my kisses planted on her nose with a saintly tolerance,
Turning her head just a little to the side,
Eyes closed and upslanting;
Who licks my beard with the rasp of her tongue if I catch her
            in a grooming frenzy,
Who leaps to my chest and places a single and talonless pad
            on my lips
If I whistle, who, if I open the door here at night as she sits in
            the chair
And walk down the path with the door left open, follows –
I see, looking back, her small head turned
Round the door edge, peering;
'Where are you going without me?' her look implies;
She cannot resist the magnetic night.

Mornings, when she squeezes somehow through the left-ajar
            window, over the sink in the kitchen,
And her ears spring up as they clear the pane-rim,
Her forepaws hooked on the window's edge, her hind legs
            clawing for purchase on the pane outside,
Just at the point when she's stuck half out, half-in,
I kiss her on the nose when she is most helpless,
And laugh, yet realise too, with the strange wild gleam in her
            eye as she comes in,
How that must seem to a bird in a tree hole,
As if the kitchen here were a giant tree-hole, and she coming in
            with me as her prey . . .

She arrives in my forest of books from the wood's
        university;
I lift her, sniffing wet mud on her paws from the miles
        of night-fields;
Counties of leafage upflourish in my mind when I
        sniff her fur
Which, lustrously white on her paws, with a pale-gold
        tinge,
Is exactly like that on the old seed heads of the Spear
        Thistle
In forgotten corners of September fields.

Now the neighbours smile as they pass, at my accepting
        time.

She follows me out when I go to the tap on this hill for
        water,
At a certain speed in her walk her tail stands up with a
        little crook at the tip,
Or she'll be in spirited mood, bouncing about on her
        flexible spine; a strange thing,
She alone
(As we all are in the end), sistered by shadow,
Leaping in gaiety in the light of the catless moon.

Gerry Cambridge (b.1959)

Little Drama

A bonny night. I step outside and gaze,
Head back in autumn dark, up into space,
Where stars between the clouds burn with quiet praise,
And think for whatever reason of your face.

Fine thoughts below those glittering Pleiades.
Regrets. Goodbyes. The largeness of the night
Summons easy nostalgia for futilities,
Free from the searching glare of window light.

But what's this, suddenly, about my feet,
Rubbing at my ankles? It's the old, fat black tom
Unusually affectionate, startling from
Revery, ragged-eared, with his small thunder.
Is it mere love, or food he wants, I wonder?
His presence somehow makes the night complete.

Gerry Cambridge (b.1959)

The Cameronian Cat

There was a Cameronian cat
   Was hunting for a prey,
And in the house she catch'd a mouse,
   Upon the Sabbath day.

The Whig, being offended
   At such an act profane,
Laid by his book, the cat he took,
   And bound her in a chain.

'Thou damn'd, thou cursed creature,
   This deed so dark with thee,
Think'st thou to bring to hell below,
   My holy wife and me?

Assure thyself, that for the deed
   Thou blood for blood must pay,
For killing of the Lord's own mouse
   Upon the Sabbath-day.'

The presbyter laid by the book,
   And earnestly he pray'd,
That the great sin the cat had done
   Might not on him be laid.

And straight to execution
    Poor baudrons she was drawn,
And high hang'd up upon a tree;
    Mess John he sung a psalm.

And when the work was ended,
    They thought the cat near dead;
She gave a paw, and then a mew,
    And stretched out her head.

'Thy name,' said he, 'shall certainly
    A beacon still remain,
A terror unto evil ones,
    For evermore. Amen.'

(ed. James Hogg, 1770⁄1835)

Towards the End

A wrecked street⁄cat got up
and shadowed us, came home
and sat an hour on your lap
in the laundry cupboard.

You counted the lice
that massed on her shoulders,
dispassionate, calm
as a man from the census.

We made her live for a while,
had her sprayed and injected,
swaddled her stiff in a towel
as a mummy;

forced milky drugs
through her shut wax mouth.
You stroked her vellum throat
with one finger, put her shaking

and small in my arms as a bird.
She pushed out a paw
as if promising something.
We smiled when she purred.

And woke in the night
to modest hoarse snorings,
fine scratchings in corners,
her peppery smell; to an itch

on our hands that matched,
palm to palm, that reddened
and spread, opened, bled.
Ringworm, they said. Then worse,

quickly worse: a shriek like brakes
skidding, wet sick on the carpet,
queer lucid red, one bony worm
that uncoiled to a comma.

You shrugged when I screamed,
cleared it bent-shouldered,
laid her flat on the floor
as a joke-cat, steam-rollered,

but her breath kept coming,
kept lifting her skin worn loose
as a dust-rag. She was light,
she was just greasy bones in a bag.

I called to her, called *baby*, *love*,
reached for your hand. She made
a rusty choking sound, squeezed out
a last tiny shit like a stone, then

you turned away I think,
I know I cried.
There was not enough between us
to keep a cat alive.

Kate Clanchy (b.1965)

Visitation

In pride of place on my work⁄surface
are an inkwell of weighted glass

and a black quill⁄pen, presented to me
when I left long⁄term employ;

a discarded life I heed less
and less, as the years pass.

But every so often with a hoarse *kraaa*
there squats on the sill a hoodie crow,

a gap in one wing where a primary
feather is missing. Teetering raggedly

it fixes me with a bloodshot eye
then flops, disgruntled, away.

Whether intent on repossessing
what belongs to it, or chastising

me for treating its lost quill
simply as a glossy symbol,

I recognise in it the beast
of conscience come home to roost.

The cat meantime sits by the fireplace,
content that nothing is amiss.

Stewart Conn (b.1936)

Cat and Water

Our thirsty cat is in the bath
lapping the puddle that squats around the plug-hole.
I turn the tap on slowly –
letting out a steady stream
but not enough to startle her.
She drinks and drinks as though she'll never stop.
Then sits up to watch the water.

It falls in a single uninterrupted flow.
A rapier you'd swear was welded metal
from tap to drain.
Or a glassy rope for a glassy snake to climb.
Mysterious, sinister, thin.
The cat replies to her own unspoken question
and probes it with a forepaw.

O now the sword's a shoal of plunging fish
and smallfry jitterbug off shrugged fur.
Again and again
her claws comb and card it like yarn,
unravelling it in twigs and sprays of light.
She frays the rope in a scatter of seeds
or sways it to a whispery rush of sound.

She knows
what we forget.
She knows this stuff's alive.
Dear beautiful prey to be caught and held and let go and
        held again.
And when I turn off the tap and she quits the bath
she leaves by way of a blackberry-path of her own.

Anna Crowe (b.1945)

The Fox and the Cat: A Fable

The Fox and the Cat, as they travell'd one day,
With moral discourse cut shorter the way:
''Tis great (says the Fox) to make justice our guide!'
'How godlike is mercy!' Grimalkin reply'd.

　Whilst thus they proceeded, a Wolf from the wood,
Impatient of hunger, and thirsting for blood,
Rush'd forth as he saw the dull shepherd asleep,
And seiz'd for his supper an innocent Sheep.

'In vain, wretched victim, for mercy you bleat,
When mutton's at hand, (says the Wolf) I must eat.'
Grimalkin's astonish'd, the Fox stood aghast,
To see the fell beast at his bloody repast.

'What a wretch, (says the Cat) 'tis the vilest of brutes:
Does he feed upon flesh, when there's herbage, and
　　roots?'
Cries the Fox, 'While our oaks give us acorns so good,
What a tyrant is this, to spill innocent blood?'

　Well, onward they march'd, and they moraliz'd still,
'Till they came where some poultry pick'd chaff by a
　　mill;
Sly Reynard survey'd them with gluttonous eyes,
And made (spite of morals) a pullet his prize.

A Mouse too, that chanc'd from her covert to stray,
The greedy Grimalkin secur'd as her prey.

A Spider that sat in her web on the wall,
Perceiv'd the poor victims, and pity'd their fall;
She cry'd, 'Of such murders how guiltless am I!'
So ran to regale on a new taken fly.

Moral
The faults of our neighbours with freedom we blame,
But tax not ourselves, tho' we practise the same.

John Cunningham (1729-1773)

Apart

We sit around a few heaped coals of fire.
Outside the summer rain drenches
Leaves, grass, brown lilac,
The spring is done and summer hesitates
Between.

They are talking among themselves
Of how to live and how to work and
How they do. Nice people all, their
Words vibrate through the quiet room.
Everything matters.

On the hearthrug, the cat
Opens one yellow eye and yawns and
Stretches a skittish armoured paw.
She does not care, she does not give a
Damn. Defends herself, contained.

And I? I am here between the two.
My head is full of sweet summer rain
And I am thinking of you.
I am thinking of you.

Catherine Czerkawska (b.1950)

An Edinburgh Cat

There are cats in the Canongate and cats in the Cowgate
   Up and down Lawnmarket and right round St Giles;
Urban cats in Trinity and rural cats at Howgate,
   Toms and tabbies purr and prowl for miles and miles and miles;
But not a single cat of them, climbs where I wait
   High in Ramsay Garden, clinging to the tiles.

From there I peer at Edinburgh with eager eyed felinity.
   Traffic and humanity, at work and sleep and play,
How my whiskers twitch at their ceaseless peregrinity
   From West End to Waverley, from Sun. to Saturday;
All the chase and chatter of the city's femininity
   On bargain hunt at Jenners, and Binns, and C. & A.

Storm clouds over Fife; in the Firth the white spray curling;
   Loud with the north easter, I shriek a merry mew;
Summer time in Princes Street; kilted dancers whirling
   Where the flowery gardens hear my purring all night thro',
Bagpipes on the Esplanade, and high above their skirling,
   I sing in shrill cacophony my joy at the Tattoo.

Greyfriars Bobby sits smug beside his Candlemakers,
   A burgess and a movie star, grown pompous by renown;
The unicorn of Mercat Cross mounts guard on holy acres,
   Law-abiding citizens who view me with a frown;
Yet if I ever fall victim to town planners and house-breakers,
   My loss would be catastrophe for Edinburgh town.

M.L. Dalgleish

Wee Plebs (Rome)

Feral
  felines
fuck and
  fight
amongst the weeds
  in Trajan's Forum.
Toppled columns
  Corinthian jigsaw.
Puddles from the
  morning rain.

They make their nests
  in holes in
the walls.
  Build their empires.
Rise.
  Fall.
Hiss and spit
  for a piece
of space.

  Up on the walkways
women and men
  holding hands,
gazing in eyes,

kissing lips,
holding tits,
  are unaware of
the epic tale
  unfolding
below them,
  all their lives.
Thousands of
  cars go round
and
  round.

Archaeologists,
  huffing
and puffing,
  try to explain,
make it fit.

  Breath falls.
Breath
  rises.

Cats and dossers
    doze in the shade,
lick their wounds,
    do it again.
Make new enemies,
    invade territories.
Hump and howl,
    hope
for the
    best.

Graham Fulton (b.1959)

Remainders

As I heave the hoover gadget about
a tiny whiteness attracts my eye.
I stoop to lift a single whisker
stuck at the foot of the skirting board
beneath the window, in the lounge.
My little cat, dead for years.

Avoiding the housework. All this time
among the crumbs, the skin and fluff,
occasional crispies and shrivelled peas.
Remainders that we never see.

Reminders we are less than perfect,
less than the sum of what we believe.

A finely tapering thread of thin.
It brings it back, the things we slip
as life cleans up; baffling love
for green eyes, a tail, a grape-sized brain.
Instinct signals, redundant words,
a bell round her neck to warn the birds.

It will go in the box that held her ash,
along with her name tag, shred of claw.
Essential, sentimental guff.
Resistance against the unforgiving
sweeping away of everything
that's ever been, will never be.

Graham Fulton (b.1959)

Black Cat Boy

he jumps off
  the cattery roof
towing a bin liner
  parachute
looking north
  into the distance
to Cat Craig and the sea.

but the boy and cat
  lived in town before:
when she was just
  a kitten
she was trapped
  in a tenement blaze
the firecat
  with a white scar
beside her eye
  the flame fleck
the seed of change.

now summer rays
  shine on them
lying in the field
  while behind him
the hills stretch

shoulder and hill
in a seamless flow
Lawmurmairz Lawmurmairz
   seen from
   below.

black cat guardian
   of darkness
goes for walks in the day
   follows him everywhere
has had two litters
   leaps on feathers
and catches
   mouse and mole.

he knows her sound
   under Blaik Law
her rasp of a purr
   dark drones
all the way
   round Boonslie Shank
Lawmurmairz Lawmurmairz
what he likes best about her:
   the face she makes
when she goes to sleep.

Valerie Gillies (b.1948)

Spell to Change Into a Cat and Back

I sall goe in till ane catt,
With sorrow, and sych, and a blak shot!
And I shall goe in the Divellis nam,
Ay quill I com hom again!

Catt, catt, God send thee a blak shott!
I was a catt just now
Bot I sal be in a woman's liknes evin now.
Catt, catt, God send thee a blak shot!

Isobel Gowdie (c.1632–1632)

Master Cat and Master Me Do Antoine Ó máille

The way I see it is that Master
Me is falling out with Servant
Me and understairs is live
With small complaints and clattering.

The dust is being too quickly
Feathered off my dear objects.
On the other hand I find myself
Impeded where I want to go.

Even the cat (He has no name.)
Is felinely aware that Master
House's bosom is not what
It used to be. The kitchen door

Swings on its hinges singing on
A foreign pitch. The mice have new
Accents and their little scurries
Have acquired a different grace.

At this time the light is always
Anxious to go away. The mantel
Brasses flicker and Malcolm Mooney's
Walrus tooth gleams yellow.

Who let you in? Who pressed
The cracked Master's cup on you?
I will show you out through
The Master's door to the Servant world.

Dont let Master Cat out.
He has to stay and serve with me.
His Master now must enter
The service of the Master Sea.

W.S. Graham (1918-1986)

On a Cat, Ageing

He blinks upon the hearth-rug,
And yawns in deep content,
Accepting all the comforts
That Providence has sent.

Louder he purrs, and louder,
In one glad hymn of praise
For all the night's adventures,
For quiet, restful days.

Life will go on for ever,
With all that cat can wish:
Warmth and the glad procession
Of fish and milk and fish.

Only – the thought disturbs him –
He's noticed once or twice,
The times are somehow breeding
A nimbler race of mice.

Alexander Gray (1882-1968)

In the same way

In the same way she cries at the kitchen door
and I slip her and she runs into circular squalls of rain

and she cries at the kitchen door
with snailtracks of rain in her muscular fur
so I open up and she runs in singing

and she cries at the kitchen door
so I open up and she crouches
then sprints into the wind

and the wind cries at the kitchen door
so I open up and call and call

and she doesn't run in but the wind does,
with rain, a squall of claws —

in the same dogged, idiotic way
I open up, send Goodnight across the brae,

and the wind canters in
and she with a wild carol

and all the night hail
melted gleaming in her furs

Jen Hadfield (b.1978)

Cat in the Apple Tree

When, for the umpteenth time he's outflitted
within paw's reach of the taunting bird, heart
goes out to him — his folly, persistence,
trapeze artiste's brilliance. 'Wings? Flight?'
you can hear him thinking, 'Who could believe it?'

Cat, all us outreach workers crouched
in the blossoming foliage of our head-sets
are up there with you. Obsessed. Deluded.
Still hoping. Did God say something just then?
Was that a poem flew by? Tomorrow we'll catch it.

Diana Hendry (b.1941)

Taking Care of Fear

This is the stray who's moved in
through the garage, who you came upon
night after night, hiding under the car
whenever you tried to go out.

You've done the right thing –
keeping the back door open, turning
your back, busying yourself at the cooker,
so it could shoot past, undisturbed.

Now it's settled inside, you can go out,
escape now and again. But when you come home
sit next to it on the sofa, even though
its waking hours are unpredictable.

Watch it doze, stretch out its paws.
Beware of its claws; they can lash out,
scratch you when you least expect.
They are sharpened daily on the glassy future.

Bring your hand – the whole of it,
not just your fingertips – down the length
of its back (be wary of the whip of the tail).
Don't hesitate, be gentle. It will accept your touch,

without comment. After many nights
settled on the sofa, you'll take up
these ministrations without thinking.
Afterwards, nothing will have changed.

Fear is still there and so are you.
But the evenings have become warmer
and you will notice unfamiliar muscles in your arm.
They might feel a little strained, sore even.

Kate Hendry (b.1970)

'Gib Hunter, Our Jolie Cat'

(from *The Taill of the Uponlandis Mous and the Burges Mous*)

With fair tretie yit scho gart hir upryse,
And to the burde thay went and togidder sat,
And scantlie had thay drunkin anis or twyse,
Quhen in come Gib Hunter, our jolie Cat,
And bad God speid; the burges up with that,
And till her hole scho went as fire on flint;
Bawdronis the uther be the bak hes hint.

Fra fute to fute he kest hir to and fra,
Quhylis up, quhylis doun, als cant as ony kid;
Quhylis wald he lat hir rin under the stra,
Quhylis wald he wink, and play with her buk heid.

Thus to the selie mous grit pane he did,
Quhill at the last, throw fortune and gude hap,
Betwix ane burde and the wall scho crap.

Syne up in haist behind ane parraling
Scho clam so hie, that Gilbert micht not get hir,
And be the clukis craftelie can hing,
Till he wes gane; hir cheir wes all the better.
Syne doun scho lap quhen thair wes nane to let hir,
And to the burges mous loud can scho cry,
'Fairweill, sister, thy feist heir I defy!

Thy mangerie is mingit all with cair,
Thy guse is gude, thy gansell sour as gall.
The subcharge off they service is bot sair;
Sa sall thow find heir efterwart na fall.
I thank yone curtyne and yone perpall wall
Of my defence now fra yone crewell beist.
Almichtie God, keip me fra sic ane feist!'

Robert Henryson (c.1420–c.1490)

Nellie's Lament for the Pirnhouse Cat
Killed by the Elevator, C........e Factory, Dundee

Oh! fareˏyeˏweel my bonnie cat,
Nae mair I'll smooth yer skin sae black.
Mony a time I stroked yer back,
  Puir wee creator;
Ye've gane yer last lang sleep tae tak'.
  The Elevator

Has sent ye aff tae your lang hame,
Whaur hunger ne'er will jag yer wame,
Whaur ye shall ne'er put in a claim
  For meal or milk;
Yer in the 'pond', free frae a' blame,
  Boiled like a whelk.

Puir hapless beast, what was't that took
Ye hunting into yon dark nook?
Whaur 'Death' sat cooring wi' his hook
  Tae nip yer neck.
I'll think upon yer deein' look
  Wi' sad respect.

My very brain ran roon about
When I saw Archie tak' ye oot,
Wi' scalped pow and bluidy snoot.

Heigh, when I think,
A stane tied roon yer neck, nae doot
    Tae gar ye sink.

Jist yesterday, my bonnie beast,
I held ye close unto my breast;
When, ye as proud as ony priest,
    Did cock yer lug;
Syne aff ye ran tae get a feast
    Frae yer milk mug.

But noo nae mair in oor pirnhouse
Ye'll hunt the rats, nor catch a moose,
Nor on the counter sit fu' douse,
    And mew and yell.
And shoot yer humph sae prude and spruce
    At rhyming Nell.

Your race upon the earth was ran,
Puir puss, ere it was weel began;
Ye've gane whaur beastie, boy, and man
    Are doomed tae go.
Omnipotence in His vast plan
    Ordained it so.

There's nane has deign'd tae mourn ye here,
Unless mysel' wi' grief sincere;

Though but a cat I'll still revere
        Thy worth wi' pity.
And ower yer memory drap a tear,
        Puir wee cheetie.

Ellen Johnston, 'The Factory Girl' (c.1835–1873)

The Nine Lives of the Cat Mandu

When I was born
I was a familiar,
a black cat, Satan's favourite form.

Next life – I was in a room
you couldn't swing a cat in.
Outside it was raining cats and dogs.

It was a small house in a mews.
Soon I was like a cat on hot bricks,
like a cat on a hot tin roof –

until I fell off and landed on my feet.
I was sleek, sly, mysterious.
I was the cat's pyjamas.

I set the cat among the pigeons.
I let the cat out of the bag.
One night, playing cat and mouse,

I lost a life under a white car,
my own dead form lit up by cat's eyes.
I came back ginger with long whiskers.

I escaped a catalogue of catastrophes.
I had good lives. I was worshipped
in Ancient Egypt. I was a Siamese,

a Manx, a sphinx, a Persian, a Burmese.
I lived lives of exquisite ease –
until I had bad catarrh in Catalonia.

I purred a catechism, prayed for baptism,
but fell into a catatonic state. No cat nap –
I was kaput. Capisch? My final date.

Jackie Kay (b.1961)

Sam and Jock the Lallans Cats

A cat o' twa score year an' ten
Sam wis reared at Ettrick Pen;
I dinna ken frae whaur Jock cam'
But baith luve Scotland as their hame
An' think McCat the finest name.
Sam has black fur and Jock is red
As rocks alang the River Jed.
Thae twa are keen on politics
An' they hae never been in breeks.
Convertit first by readin' *Smeddum*
They set the cause o' Scotland's freedom
In front o' Tory or Communist
(Yon lads are faur owre opportunist!)
Sam frae *The Scotscat* taks his sclent
An' Jock says Sam's views are weel meant.
Auld Sam says Keengs and Queens are grand,
But Jock is mair Republican
Wi' veesions o' a Promised Lan'.
Sae when he gaes doon by the Mound
For him the Left Wing case is sound.
The verra thocht o't Sam annoys,
He cries the oratory – 'Noise!'
At Scotland's wrangs thegither raiket
He a' but bust his Sunday jaiket,
But canna thole kenspeckle ploys

By the United Scotland boys,
By Wendy Wood, or black-vised Young;
He says that Duggie sud be hung,
A runclewit he wis an' clairty
Tae jine the English Labour Pairty!
When speakers glower wi' risin' voices
As Free Cats analyse ilk Crisis,
Jock has an ear for their surmises.
Tae pit a wheen o' points a' ettle
Bilin' an' splutterin' like a kettle:
'Gowdfish are mair nor Fort Knox metal.'
An' Jock wi' his impident stare
Shouts 'Suas Alba' and 'Hear, Hear.'
'Kittlins an' cats are all aware
Tae mak domestic hollow-ware
That wis the anerly use allowed
In More's *Utopia* for gowd.'
Sam gulps, 'Whit mair can ye expect
Wi' a Scots business bottlenecked?'
An' Jock pits in, lik a wee tartar,
Gif Scots wad trade abroad by barter
We'd a' be dressed in furs and nylons
An' hae oor halidays in the Hielan's.
Instead o' leevin' in semi-famine
We'd whop up grouse an' fush for salmon.
It wad restore oor confidence
Sharely it's anely commonsense?'
Jock lea's Scots Secretariat books;

An' though he's jined the Scots Convention,
He says, 'In wars, non-intervention
By Scots micht help tae ease the tension.'

Archie Lamont (1907-1975)

Between Two Worlds

Every morning at nine, past my window
Woofles, the affectionate Persian cat,
creeps along the line of his own balance
paw upon paw, as if afraid of his weight.

Known only to Woofles, the line stretches through
a hole in the dyke, into the wood beyond,
where mice flicker like leaves, and baby rabbits
listen, as if by their own foolishness stunned.

There's nothing to hear, except the blundered dog
barking at distance that it can't leap through
to leave the pampered time of humans. Meanwhile
the line's run out as far as it need go.

Mouse or baby rabbit never knows
what the pounce came from. Scuffle or squeak
as instinct wills, the yellow eyes burn,
the teeth rend and crunch, the small bones break.

Having rolled up the slackened line on whiskers
scentlessly clean, a jump back out of his skulk,
and there, without a hint of blood still warm,
is pussy, round your ankles after milk.

Maurice Lindsay (1918–2009)

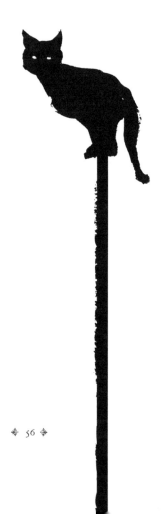

Fourteen Ways of Touching the Peter

I

You can push
your thumb
in the
ridge
between his
shoulder-blades
to please him.

II

Starting
at its root,
you can let
his whole
tail
flow
through your hand.

III

Forming
a fist
you can let
him rub
his bone
skull
against it, hard.

IV

When he makes
bread,
you can lift
him
by his under-
sides on your
knuckles.

V

In hot
weather
you can itch
the fur
under
his chin. He
likes that.

VI

At night
you can hoist
him
out of his bean-stalk,
sleepily
clutching
paper bags.

VII
Pressing
his head against
your cheek,
you can carry
him
in the dark,
safely.

VIII
In late Autumn
you can find
seeds
adhering
to his fur.
There are
plenty.

IX
You can prise
his jaws
open,
helping
any medicine
he won't
abide, go down.

X

You can touch
his
feet, only
if
he is relaxed.
He
doesn't like it.

XI

You can comb
spare thin
fur
from his coat,
so he won't
get
fur-ball.

XII

You can shake
his rigid
chicken-leg leg,
scouring his
hind-quarters
with his Vim
tongue.

XIII

Dumping
hot fish
on his plate, you can
fend
him off,
pushing
and purring.

XIV

You can have
him shrimp
along you,
breathing,
whenever
you want
to compose poems.

George MacBeth (1932-1992)

To the Flea, Combed from My Cat's Back

Arrested integrity, set
   into the tight hedge
   of what he has,
I mean whatever ails
   when he sweats,

orb of blood, lewd,
   with the quick ichor
   of his glory's breast-bones,
chicken-skin,
   already sickening

towards the latter end
   of all cats,
   and of such even
as you, sire,
   cracknell of sparkling,

trailer of ire at
   which all stare
   bemused, fearful
of what may start,
   thickened, from your place

in the sun of his body, I
   pray you be peaceful
   to him,
and to us all,
   for her sake, whom I love.

George MacBeth (1932–1992)

The Cat

Looking up from what I'm doing
(looking up a word, to find out
if it means what I *want* it to . . .)
I find out it's me who's been
looked up – by the unexpected:
outside my window, looking in
is a fat, striped Amazement.
I see myself as I'm seen
by this startled incarnation:
in his eyes' mad, golden moons
there's terror – and recognition.
And I see what I mean to him
whether I want to or not:
man, in his undergrowth of words,
hunting a wild connotation . . .
As I close the curtains on him,
he turns on his tail's questionmark
and leaps into a starless dark
night full of desperate definitions.

Brian McCabe (b. 1951)

Black Cat in a Morning

Black cat, slink longer: flatten through the grass.
The chaffinch scolds you, pebbling you with chinks
Of quartzy sound, where the green lilac banks
White falls of stillness and green shades of peace.

A shape where topaz eyes may climb and find
The fluttering gone, the dust smelling of green,
The green a royal *deshabille* of the sun
Tossed on a tree and stitched with its own gold.

And chaffinch rattling from another bush
Shakes with his furious ounce a yard of leaves,
Strikes flints together in his soft throat and moves
In out, out in, two white stripes and a blush.

Black cat pours to the ground, is pool, is cat
That walks finicking away, twitching behind
A stretched foot: sits, is carved, upon the ground,
Drubbing soft tomtoms in his silky throat.

He changes all around him to his scale.
Suburban suns are jungle stripes of fire
And all the mornings that there ever were
Make this one mount and mount and overspill.

And in their drenching where time cannot be,
Amiably blinking in ancestral suns
He swallows chaffinches in stretching yawns
And holds the world down under one soft paw.

Norman MacCaig (1910-1996)

Connoisseurs

Under a tree I read a Latin book,
And there, in seeming slumber, lies my cat;
Each of us thinking, with our harmless look,
Of this and that.

Such singing — prettier than any words —
O singers you are sweet and well-to-do!
My cat, who has the finest taste in birds,
Thinks so too.

Dugald S. MacColl (1859-1948)

Claire with the hindlegs

Claire with the hindlegs of Ginger
her cat friend dragging along the carpet
as she held him and hauled him
into her world of feline language.
He accepted all that

but finally taught her
smart cat
to speak human.

James McGonigal (b.1947)

The Old Tom Cat *(Air: The Ivy Green)*

A downy cove is our old tom cat,
  Just turned thirty years old;
He eateth the lean, and leaveth the fat,
  And won't touch his meals when too cold.
His food must be crumbled, and not decay'd,
  To pleasure his dainty whim,
But a turkey bone from the kitchen-maid,
  Is a very good meal for him.

Chorus: Creeping over the tiles pit pat,
      A downy cove is the old tom cat.

Whole joints have fled, and their bones decayed,
   And dishes have broken been,
But old tom still follows the kitchen-maid,
   And slyly licks up the cream.
Now, old tom cat, in his lonely days,
   Shall joyously think of the past,
And a big leg of mutton, that never was touched,
   Shall be food for our Tommy at last.

Chorus: Creeping over the tiles pit pat,
      A downy cove is the old tom cat.

Fast creepeth he, though he hath no wings,
   And a sly old dodger is he,
As under the garret window he sings –
   Ain't you coming out tonight, love, to me?
Then slyly he creepeth the gutters all round,
   And his old tail he joyously waves,
As his lady love from a garret he spies,
   And he sings her his amorous staves.

Chorus: Creeping over the tiles pit pat,
      A downy cove is the old tom cat.

Paddy McGown (1855; *birth and death dates not known*)

My Cat Asleep

My cat sleeps on the windowsill.
She is a soft lump, a small heap of fur,
all shape and all resistance gone;
a black fur candle might have come to her
if one had left it too long in the sun.
Almost I feel she could dissolve,
run off in furry streams,
black waters no one but herself would dare to fish,
to hook up on the bank, as she hooks now,
wish after bloody wish, the easy meat of dreams.

Yet darkness claws a foothold
from the brightest sky
and definition with the mice returns;
far down within the sleeping heart of her,
nine times unquenchable,
a lunatic ambition burns.
Soon she will wake and firm herself and go
to where in a little ecstasy
the daring mouse runs to and fro.
How naturally she works!
She is as much a part of her vocabulary then
as is the sailor gone to sea.
And I too have a catskin to put on,
for so I sleep and wake
and so the poem emerges and desires me.

Alasdair Maclean (1926-1994)

A Strange Cat Got In

When we arrived home, the wooden cherub on
  the mantelpiece had fallen and broken a
  leg. Our cat would not have done that.
  There was a tumbler chopped in two. Nor
  that either. In the kitchen the bucket
  had bent sideways, and the bathroom wash⁄
  basin was choked with fragments of scent.
  Nor that; nor that; nor that. A strange
  cat had got in.
What's the matter with the boy these days?
  He used to sunfire his mouth, ever, from
  his potting and cotted days. Would chatter
  what he did or required to do. Would rest
  his head on my knee like a falling star.
  But now he sits glooming along vacuity:
  and if he seldom looks, he sees often out⁄
  side the house. A strange cat got in.
They do not build houses now, nor motorcars,
  nor shape shoes, as was. There is always
  noise of much moving, in day streets and
  night rooms. We can hardly think any more:
  it is all processed for us. Even Charity
  is superannuated by the State. We can barely
  give to the other poor. A strange cat got in.
We remember the early run up to midnight,
  scramblings over roofs, secrecies next day.

We remember when we raced and were naturesome.
Something must have been loose in us,
something open to abscess, and a strange
cat got in. We have to lock our souls up
now before we go to bed, and to insure
our tickets of tomorrow morning.
Once, thinking I had trapped the intruder,
I hesitated between watering-can and
walking-stick. When I returned from this
indecision, it was my wife's black jumper,
slipped from the supper-table. How long
has my wife liked to wear black? How
long has she stopped redding up the house
when there was no more rush to bed?
We never knew how much more we could live.
Wars took the cement out of our new
foundations, and tangled the wires of our
extensions, how many years ago? Now it
is idle to dream when there is no more
time for hope: but there is eagerness to
dream. Only to dream. And our dreams
have to go backward.
Did a strange cat get in? Maybe it did.
But to you it was a friend and usual cat.

Joseph Gordon Macleod (1903-1984)

Catfish

Almost uglier than a monk,
A catfish, with a massive head
And flapping tail, unable to be
Contained within the framework
Of a wooden crate. Garnished

With light, its rough-grained
Skin, a lunar blue, glows above
Handfuls of manufactured ice.
Warily, a young boy pokes his
Fist into the dog-toothed mouth.

Myopic eyes stare back at his
Unnecessary doubts. In the oily
Stench of the harbour a family cat
Has drowned. It floats face-down
Amongst discarded rubber gloves

And crushed tin-cans. Peering
Into cloudy water, all its pickled
Eyes can see, is the same as the
Catfish saw on the cluttered quay –
Death's five-fingered hand –

The invisible grip of the sea.

Gordon Meade (b.1957)

Bully Cat

Bully Cat
is very fat
and smelly

his body
is mostly
his belly

Bully Cat
is lazy
and nasty

lying down
he's like a crazy
Cornish pasty

Bully Cat
despises
his owner

he eats her food
but deep down
he's a loner

Bully Cat
is very far
from housetrained

and further still
from bird⁄trained
or mouse⁄trained

for Bully Cat
will go where
he pleases

and every time
he kills something
he teases!

Bully Cat
is merciless
to other cats

to smaller cats
and kitten cats
and mother cats

and as for dogs,
well, Bully Cat
dismisses them!

he spits them
he claws them
he hisses them!

Bully Cat
tattoos those
who mess with him

so children tend
to play less
and less with him

Bully Cat
bit a girl
who kissed him

he died last week
and no one
missed him.

Richard Medrington (b.1956)

The Cat

There once was a French cat called Sappho
Who cried out, 'Souris à l'échafaud!'
But the mice whistled back
'Mets la chatte dans le sac!'
And they dragged her away with a gaffeau.

Edwin Morgan (1920–2010)

Like, Little Russian Cat

KAKKOTE
HOKKAKK
OTEHOKK
AKKOTEH
OKKAKKO
TEHOKKA
KKOTEHO
KKAKKOT
EHOKKAK
KOTEHOK

Edwin Morgan (1920–2010)

Scotch Cat

chee
  chee
    cheetikiepu
    ssiecheetik
    iepussieche
    etikiepussi
    echeetikiep
    ussiecheeti
    kiepussiech
    eetikiepuss
    iecheetikie
    pussiecheet
    ikiepussiec
    heetikiepus
    siecheetiki
    epussiechee
          chee
           chee

Edwin Morgan (1920–2010)

Three Cats

FRENCH ROCKET CAT OCTOBER 1963

oh là‑haut
spacecat
saharapara
chatsauf
mieux

GONE CAT

say cheese
yes mite
cheshire
take that
grin off your
hey –

ROYAL PREROGATIVE CAT

I am
as I am
E's cat

Edwin Morgan (1920‑2010)

Lines on a Bird and Cat Show in Glasgow

Prizes awarded by a Clergyman from England

Stand by your points upon the line,
　　Let every hand be steady;
Send an express, an' lose nae time,
　　For, losh! the cats are ready.

Wi' glossy hair an' skin sae clean,
　　Quite free frae a' infection,
They gaze upon the motley scene
　　While waiting for inspection.

Should cats, like men, feel discontent,
　　It's from their want o' knowledge;
They little ken their judge was sent
　　Five sessions tae the college.

The *Herald* tak's the greatest pains
　　To tell us what they're doing;
The Lancers' band plays stirring strains
　　To keep the cats frae mewing.

What comfort tae a country cat
　　This day will be afforded,
That cleric hands did weigh an' pat,
　　And a' her worth recorded.

Nae tortoise‑shell need thraw her face,
　　Nor whine about her kitten;
In history's page she'll find a place
　　Where births and deaths are written.

Wi' glee may puss noo whisk her tail –
　　What tongue dare noo deride her;
She's higher in the social scale
　　Than many a poor backslider.

O' honours cats hae got their fill,
　　Conferred by our Directors,
Wha yet may fix on Gilmore Hill
　　A chair for cat inspectors.

The press does often raise the cry,
　　That poor folks are neglected;
Now cats in concert may reply,
　　They're ten‑fold mair respected.

How happy is the shepherd's state
　　Whose flock needs no direction,
Who can his talents dedicate
　　To bird and cat inspection.

Thus far an' wide has spread his fame,
  How wives their cats may fatten;
An' styles it by some honour'd name,
  In Hebrew, Greek, or Latin.

An' when his thread o' life's spun out,
  And judgment is suspended,
The Kirk an' cats will then cast out
  'Bout which he maist befriended.

James Munce (b.1817)

The Meenister's Cat

the inductit new minister
in her new manse study
screivin the sunday sermon
a gless muscadet aside inspirin texts
bane dry, caller an white
keeks doon an smiles upon her cat
whae curious tae see her wark saw late at een
wimples in atween warm limbs
an purrs sae deip an kirkielike
an sib untae an organ peep
that she blesses him
fae deip within her hert

fer the meenister's cat wis an angelic cat
beatific, chaste an decorous
evangelic an faithfu
guid an hummle yet infinite an joyous
the meenister's cat wis a kosher cat
leal, meek an noble
ossianic, pure an quintessential
rarified an sublime
the meenister's cat wis a transcendental cat
universal, virtuous an worshipfu
baith xenophyllic an zealous
een as he zzzzzzzzzzzzzzzzzzzzzzzed
dreamin on spuggies an meece
he wizzzzz

th'aul din meenister man
plankit his lane ben the victorian bing
he cudnae cry his ain
drafty an stoorie an as guddled as a Kafka castle
thinks on sermons past
that he can resurrect athoot yerkin
his elders fae their doucie dwams,
tae yaise as a closing text
afore he caas a curtain
ower his lang career,
an as he gethers the menses yet his
tae gar the daurk an daurkening dram
tae his dry an drucken lips
aul baudrons smools thro wuiden legs
wi liftit tail an rig bane bou'd
narries its sleekit een
an commends his sowel tae hell
sssssssssssssssssssssssssscraichin

fer the meenister's cat wis an atheist,
a bastard cat an a calvinist
baith diabolical an dour
evil, fushonless an grim
the meenister's cat wis a harem cat
iconoclastic an but a Jezebel,
Judas an Janus
forby a kelpie's cat
baith lewd an libidinous

the minister's cat wis a malagrugous nihilist
obsequious an perverted
querulous, randy an satanic
thrawn, ugsome, vengefu an wicked
the minister's cat wis an X certificate cat
ootae some zombie film
that ZZZZZZZZZZZZZZZZZZZZZZZZPAT at him
whae wis meenister

syne suddent wis dumstrucken
bi a fowertie oonse bottle
wheechin thro the air
sib untae a tongue of flame
writ large athort the lift
wappin it right atween the een
sae that it kythed a kittlin again
an the meenister spak furth sayin
that'll suffer the bugger tae cam untae me.

John Murray (b.1954)

Cat Accident

A small sad tiger, sent to sleep too young.
Behind the apple tree, just two feet deep
the ground was hard, a flintstone to my steel.
I curled his body in a last cat-sleep.

In his brown bed of earth he seemed content.
I wished him well, wherever he had gone:
into cat-nothingness or transmigration.
Hope I look half as good when I am done.

William Neill (1922-2010)

Nursery Rhymes

Poussie, poussie, baudrons,
Where hae ye been?
I've been at London
To see the queen!

Poussie, poussie, baudrons,
What got ye there?
I got a guid fat mousikie
Rinnin' up a stair!

Poussie, poussie, baudrons,
What did ye do wi't?
I put it in my meal-pock,
To eat it to my bread!

☙

Jean, Jean, Jean
The cat's at the cream,
Supping with her forefeet,
And glowering with her een.

☙

Lingle, lingle, lang tang,
Our cat's deid!
What did she die with?
With a sair heid!

All you that kent her,
When she was alive,
Come tae her burial,
Atween four and five.

☙

The grey cat's kittled in Charlie's wig,
The grey cat's kittled in Charlie's wig;
There's one of them living and two of them dead,
The grey cat's kittled in Charlie's wig.

🐾

Pussie at the fireside
    Suppin up brose,
Doon came a cinder
    And burnt pussy's nose.
Och, said pussy,
    That's no fair.
Weel, said the cinder,
    Ye shoudna been there.

🐾

The cattie rade to Paisley, to Paisley, to Paisley,
The cattie rade to Paisley upon a harrow tine;
And she came louping hame again,
And she came louping hame again,
And she came louping hame again
Upon a mare o mine.
It was upon a Wednesday,
A windy, windy Wednesday,
It was upon a Wednesday,
Gin I can rightly mind.

🐾

A cat cam fiddlin
Oot o a barn,
Wi a pair o bagpipes
Under her arm.

She cud sing naething but
'Fiddle cum fee,
The moose has mairrit
The bumble bee.'

Pipe cat,
Dance moose,
We'll hae a waddin
At oor guid hoose.

A Cat Suite

MY MOTHER AS A CAT

After my mother's funeral,
after the wake, my sister
let us choose, from several,
a tortoiseshell kitten

to accompany our children
through the quick years
to the threshold of adulthood.
Always, she has been

a dainty cat, possessing
qualities of cleanliness,
propriety, far above those
of her peers. Such that

her killing of a robin, say,
struck us as indelicate,
an unnatural affront.
But, in time, though her chin

remained blessedly white,
a wheel of bones began to show

through her haunches; her belly
fell; her sweet face

became drawn with age.
When she turned to me then,
I saw my mother without a spit
of conscious thought ⁄

it *was* my mother, the brightness
of her eyes filmed with age,
her steady gaze edged
with severity as, dear God,

it could be, when she urged me
not to disappoint. Was our cat
only briefly a host for her spirit
or has there always been

this maternal other, watching?
I spend most of the day now
in⁄house with our cat. I know
her needs for sleep; I know

her favourite spots. Mostly,
we do not bother each other.
But there are those times
when she will not settle —

when behind each door, she waits
for me, each room I enter,
she goes before me. She mews
for what I cannot provide –

for food, water, are not the answer.
Still, she persists and I think now,
not of my mother, not of the steady
mewling about death –

my mother's, the cat's, my own –
but about former lovers,
pursuing me for those times,
when I failed through neglect,

confusion, fear or casual
cruelty; reminding me
that commitment might have
safeguarded the future

in which I live, while also
debarring me from it.
She follows me, from room
to room, lest I become forgetful.

The time I could have assuaged
her hunger is long gone. Yet still
I live with a ghost's empty desires
as bones jut from ancient fur.

AND THIS IS WHEN

and this is when you are watching me before the fire and I am lying with the death-stillness on me, till I reach out a leg and my head turns with the owl-swivel, chin up, and look at the needle-tooth I show you, just there, and there again my soft chin hair, so white you snow-talk of it – and you sit with the death-stillness too, but you cannot do it as I can do it, nor can you stretch like I can stretch and, though you talk of reaching for the sky, that is the old talk; you cannot reach beyond yourself as I can reach into spaces you cannot imagine – full-stretch, I place a paw on each of the icy poles, each paw an igloo in a drift of snow and that is why the little paw-shake when they return to me and you think it is the dream-talk; whereas you, you are so folded into yourselves, the night does not wait for you, you climb no walls, you jump so small and so very long it has been since you took two steps at a time; but from high walls I land as four-square as ever; but you, oh, it is the years are catching up with you, the two legs so very tired – and though I am ancient, I am ancient in the now, for the now is where I live and no regret, for I look what memory has done to you, how memory- talk weighs you down like an extra head; I do not want to reach where you can reach, so I shall be as I always was – whereas you, oh laid low by the extra head of memory; look now how the night does not wait for you, how you struggle to keep your shoulders above the surface of the night, as you go upstairs one step at a time; while I turn again and stretch and go; believe me, I am not now lovely as I go, I am not the snow-talk any more, but the dark cannot make me nothing; see how I shake your world from me as I go, I do not even take a deep breath as night takes me.

THE CAT-POEM

And, for these weeks, the poem
  has been away. Where do poems go
   when we turn from them; stop
working at the nap of their fur;
  when their insistence has done with us?
   Is there a night they go to – the things
that live apart from us – to a world
  as forgetful of us
   as we are of it? This one
pads over the night-wet grass
  and claws its way up a wooden fence.
   Then, onto the brick wall where, briefly,
it's silhouetted against the moon
  (a cliché I'll edit out later).
   And now its life is a mystery to me.
In the silent darkness,
  it connects the silences –
   the blank windows, the pools
of forgetfulness the back gardens make.
  The presence of the cat on the arm
   of my chair does not negate
this other one whose adventures
  are stranger than I know. Often,
   it has no part of anything
I am thinking of; it has gone too far
  for me to follow. I only recognise

it has been an absence in my life
when it has returned to me,
    pestering me for what it needs;
        for what I alone can give it.

MAX

I was always back first
to that run-down house
on the edge of the marshes.
So, it was I who scrubbed

away at the cat reek –
though the lemony Vim
never managed to mask
the foul pungency

of cat shit. In the end,
I found it in the corner
of a disused cupboard –
a mound of it by then

I had to gag myself
to shift. Max, whose idea
were you? We carried you
to the small garden's end

and raced back to the house.
If we won, you'd claw up
the half-glazed door and hang,
paws and face like Kilroy,

your eyes blazing with fear.
So what did it take, Max,
for you to lose yourself
to the dark canal paths,

to the existential
wastes of Hackney Marshes?
I rarely think of you,
but, when I do, even

these forty years later,
I think how we failed you.
And when you haunt me now
it is as pure terror —

like a black nerve of flame
I cannot hold onto;
a black nerve of flame
that does not want to be held.

PEEDIE AND MOLLY

Our Peedie was shy.
The weight of a hand
brushing her side triggered
her flight. Company

held no attraction.
Your Molly? Completely
other. Raised early
with an Alsatian

she fought her corner;
lay like a slipper
before her tormentor:
till he raised his head

and she came too, neat
claws latched to his snout.
Whereas our Peedie
was over-sensitive

to our wants, Molly
butted into your hand
like a nuzzling calf,
blind to all rebuffs.

But just lately, time's
caught up with them both.
Molly has grey-scaled eyes;
both of them buttons

of bone down their backs.
They bear sudden age
with innocence: none
of the sheepish shrugs

we're tempted to give,
disclaiming our years
like a shameful old coat.
Rather, in Peedie

note the greater trust;
in Molly, the gentler
affection. Unmet
by miles all their lives,

they have somehow grown
into age, like sisters.

THE MIRACLE

And now she is a Nefertiti cat,
statuesque on the footstool before us,

as we look past her into the full bloom
of the TV. She purrs herself silent

while staring at us, as if her staring
will make the miracle happen. OK,

she says, through her faded marigold eyes,
what better time, while the moon is bright and fat,

to complete my journey to the human –
or for you to turn yourselves into cats?

GIFT

She sits on my desk, grooming;
plotting firm strokes with plenty
of follow through. She tugs

at a paw – leaves me
the nib of a hollow claw
sharp, pearled and perfect:

a sickle moon, caught
in the early morning light.

CODA

I hear the key turn,
your bag hit the floor.
Through a second door –

the illusionless
moment. Within it,
I stroke our old cat –

and I turn to you.

Tom Pow (b.1950)

The Wildcat

Today I saw a wildcat. Up the brae,
you'd think, in Landseer-painted, gloaming glen
or on some moor where tweeded gentlemen
sip from their hip-flasks at their Purdied play.
But no such thing. This wildcat stalks the street,
its yellow eyes burning with battles won.
Dark as a sandstone entry, it has run
invisibly on heavy-padded feet
through squares and closes, through launderettes and
bars,
leaving a whiff of musk, a rusty grin
and muscles moving under city skin
marked with the long, brown stripes of ancient scars.
The beast is dead, they say. And yet, those eyes
gleam in each street lamp, angry, wild and wise.

Alison Prince (b.1931)

The Twa Cats and the Cheese

Twa *Cats* anes on a *Cheese* did light,
To which baith had an equal Right;
But Disputes, sic as aft arise,
Fell out a sharing of the Prize.
Fair Play, said ane, ye bite o'er thick,
Thae Teeth of your's gang wonder quick:
Let's part it, else lang or the Moon
be chang'd, the *Kebuck* will be done.
But wha's to do't; – they're Parties baith,
And ane may do the other Skaith,
Sae with Consent away they trudge,
And laid the *Cheese* before a Judge:
A *Monkey* with a champsho Face,
Clerk to a Justice of the Peace,
A Judge he seem'd in Justice skill'd,
When he his Master's Chair fill'd;
Now Umpire chosen for Division,
Baith sware to stand by his Decision.
Demure he looks. – The *Cheese* he pales, –
He prives it good, – Ca's for the Scales;
His Knife whops throw't, – in twa it fell;
He puts ilk haff in either Shell:
Said he, We'll truly weigh the Case,
And strictest Justice shall have Place;
The lifting up the Scales, he fand
The tane bang up, the other stand:

Syne out he took the heaviest haff,
And ate a Knoost o't quickly aff,
And try'd it syne; – and now prov'd light:
Friend Cats, said he, we'll do ye right.
Then to the ither haff he fell,
And laid till't teughly Tooth and Nail,
Till weigh'd again it lightest prov'd.
The Judge wha this sweet Process lov'd,
Still weigh'd the Case, and still ate on,
'Till Clients baith were weary grown,
And tenting how the Matter went,
Cry'd, Come, come, Sir, we're baith content.
Ye fools, quoth he, and *Justice* too,
Maun be content as well as you.
Thus grumbled *they*, thus *he* went on,
Till baith the Haves were near hand done:
Poor *Pousies* now the Daffine saw
Of gawn for Nignyes to the Law;
And bill'd the Judge, that he wad please
To give them the remaining Cheese:
To which his Worship grave reply'd,
The Dues of Court maun first be paid.
Now Justice pleas'd: – What's to the fore
Will but right scrimply clear your Score;
That's our Decreet; – gae hame and sleep,
And thank us ye're win aff sae cheap.

Allan Ramsay (1684-1758)

Propinquity

is the province of cats. Living by accident,
lapping the food at hand or sleeking down
in an adjacent lap when sleep occurs to them,
never aspiring to consistency
in homes or partners, unaware of property,
cats take their chances, love by need or nearness
as long as the need lasts, as long as the nearness
is near enough. The code of cats is simply
to take what comes. And those poor souls who claim
to own a cat, who long to recognise
in bland and narrowing eyes a look like love,
are bound to suffer should they expect
cats to come purring punctually home.
Home is only where the food and the fire are,
but might be anywhere. Cats fall on their feet,
nurse their own wounds, attend to their own laundry,
and purr at appropriate times. O folly, folly,
to love a cat, and yet
we dress with love the distance that they keep,
the hair-raising way they have, and easily blame
all their abandoned litters and torn ears
on some marauding tiger, well aware
that cats themselves do not care.
Yet part of us is cat. Confess –
love turns on accident and needs
nearness; and the various selves we have

accrue from our cat-wanderings, our chance
crossings. Imagination prowls at night,
cat-like, among odd possibilities.
Only our dog-sense brings us faithfully home,
makes meaning out of accident, keeps faith,
and, cat-and-dog, the arguments go at it.
But every night, outside, cat-voices call
us out to take a chance, to leave
the safety of our baskets and to let
what happens happen. 'Live, live!' they catcall.
'Each moment is your next! Propinquity,
propinquity is all!'

Alastair Reid (b.1926)

Cat-Faith

As a cat, caught by the door opening,
on the perilous top shelf, red-jawed and
    raspberry-clawed,
lets itself fall floorward without looking,
sure by cat-instinct it will find the ground,
where innocence is; and falls
anyhow, in a furball, so fast that the eye
misses the twist and trust
that come from having fallen before,
and only notices cat silking away,
crime inconceivable in so meek a walk:

so do we let ourselves fall morningward
through shelves of dream. When, libertine at dark,
we let the visions in, and the black window
grotesques us back, our world unbalances.
Many-faced monsters of our own devising
jostle on the verge of sleep, as the room
loses its edges and grows hazed and haunted
by words murmured or by woes remembered,
till, sleep-dissolved, we fall, the known world leaves us,
and room and dream and self and safety melt
into a final madness, where any landscape
may easily curdle, and the dead cry out . . .

but ultimately, it ebbs. Voices recede.
The pale square of the window glows and stays.
Slowly the room arrives and dawns, and we
arrive in our selves. Last night, last week, the past
leak back, awake. As light solidifies,
dream dims. Outside, the washed hush of the garden
waits patiently and, newcomers from death,
how gratefully we draw its breath!
Yet, to endure that unknown night by night,
must we not be sure, with cat-insight,
we can afford its terrors, and that full day
will find us at the desk, sane, unafraid –
cheeks shaven, letters written, bills paid?

Alastair Reid (b.1926)

Curiosity

may have killed the cat. More likely,
the cat was just unlucky, or else curious
to see what death was like, having no cause
to go on licking paws, or fathering
litter on litter of kittens, predictably.

Nevertheless, to be curious
is dangerous enough. To distrust
what is always said, what seems,
to ask odd questions, interfere in dreams,
smell rats, leave home, have hunches,
does not endear cats to those doggy circles
where well-smelt baskets, suitable wives, good lunches
are the order of things, and where prevails
much wagging of incurious heads and tails.

Face it. Curiosity
will not cause us to die —
only lack of it will.
Never to want to see
the other side of the hill
or that improbable country
where living is an idyll
(although a probable hell)
would kill us all.

Only the curious
have if they live a tale
worth telling at all.

Dogs say cats love too much, are irresponsible,
are dangerous, marry too many wives,
desert their children, chill all dinner tables
with tales of their nine lives.
Well, they are lucky. Let them be
nine‑lived and contradictory,
curious enough to change, prepared to pay
the cat‑price, which is to die
and die again and again,
each time with no less pain.
A cat‑minority of one
is all that can be counted on
to tell the truth, and what cats have to tell
on each return from hell
is this: that dying is what the living do,
and that dead dogs are those who never know
that dying is what, to live, each has to do.

Alastair Reid (b.1926)

Nightlife

Dragged from that half-right, half-wrong narrative
of dream, ripped from a twisted blanket of sleep
by a commotion I can't, in the dark, identify.
With the light on, I see: the laundry basket
overturned: a sheaf of papers, torn and crumpled;
work out the culprit – he who sleeps all day
in this dark season, has had a mad turn,
flung his furry bulk about, hurdled chairs,
scaled curtains with piton claws, marauded,
his hunting instinct fired by hypothetical mice.
Now he's crashed out, burnt out, spent
beneath my night-hawk daughter's empty bed.
I light another cigarette, contemplate drifting cobwebs
on the ceiling, fail to smooth out tangled sheets
of panic, wish away the long slow hours till dawn, listen
with lessening hope, for footsteps, a key in the lock.

Dilys Rose (b.1954)

The Cat

The cat noses among my books.
It nudges Homer.
Its wedge-shaped head nuzzles Tolstoy
to scratch at its fleas.
It pushes its head past Jane Austen searching for mice.
Later it sits on my knees
serene in the warm sunshine,
then in a trice
it runs out the window and climbs up a fresh green tree.
You too were a god, weren't you, cat,
tall, aloof, ghostly, impassive as Zeus.
You too are the justice of your own grass,
the doom of the mole and the mouse.

Iain Crichton Smith (1928-1998)

The Cat

You were eighty-five when the cat appeared
one night at your door. It was perfectly white.
You wouldn't let it enter the house but you fed it
on scraps of fish which you placed on a blue plate.
It reared at your bedroom window like a stoat
mewing to get in: but you refused.
Sometimes you would threaten it with your fist.
What a strange white bony animal it was!
It would stare at you intently from the grass
and you would think: This thin beast troubles me.
My bones too are shaken as if he
were a sinister part of me, that had gone
hunting inquisitively about the stones.
The night before you died, it stared fiercely
in through the window, a tall vertical eel.
Its concentration was unshakeable.
And your bones melted and you lay at last,
a plate beside you, while your stubbly beard
had a fishy tang, wild, perilous, abhorred.

Iain Crichton Smith (1928-1998)

The Wildcat

The wildcat sits on the rock.
His hair is spitting fire
into the morning air.
His eyes are yellow.

Club-headed dynamic cat,
he is all power and force.
Among the dry green grass,
the hares are playing.

The air is clear and pure.
The hares are leaping and jumping
over invisible fences
of a pure brilliant blue.

The wildcat sits by himself
on his stony throne, not thinking.
His fur simmers like fire
snarling and sparking.

Iain Crichton Smith (1928-1998)

Stormy Day and a Cat, November

The gods is mairchin owre the roof
With ten⁄ton buits on their feet –
Valhalla houls in the lum,
Trees snap, their branches hurl
Across this high windae here . . . and
The haill world teems in a second Deluge.

I sit idle as my cat
Immobile, gazes at the interesting scene,
Intent in seeming wonder.

> ('An excellent companion for
> A literary gentleman, a cat,'
> Said fat auld Gautier,
> And, Dod, he was richt, at that.)

And sae bemusit by the storm outby,
Tak ma pen to scrieve a word t'ye,
Bypittin mair important cares
Wi the full approval o' a furry cat
That maybe kens the message
That I send, my love, sweetmeat, bluid⁄drap –
Or maybe juist is watchin
The rain dinging doun,
Blawn by gust and squalls

And great drifts o' leaves . . . leaves . . .
A million leaves, impalpable as Paradise
(As human dreams for us, *mon chat*)
Through the streamin windae in between, *hélas!*
(And could be richt, at that,
Mon Théophile, n'est-ce-pas?)

Nou the gods on the roof again . . .
Clump . . . clump . . . their ten-ton buits –
Ah me!
Come on buckle to, *mon vieux*.
Aye weill, I will. *Adieu! Adieu, cherie!*

And pray for Ptah
The Inscrutable
In Holy Egypt.
Enshallah!

Sydney Goodsir Smith (1915-1975)

Lisy's Parting with Her Cat

The dreadful hour with leaden pace approached,
Lashed fiercely on by unrelenting fate,
When Lisy and her bosom Cat must part:
For now, to school and pensive needle doomed,
She's banished from her childhood's undashed joy,
And all the pleasing intercourse she kept
With her grey comrade, which has often soothed
Her tender moments while the world around
Glowed with ambition, business, and vice,
Or lay dissolved in sleep's delicious arms;
And from their dewy orbs the conscious stars
Shed on their friendship influence benign.

But see where mournful Puss, advancing, stood
With outstretched tail, casts looks of anxious woe
On melting Lisy, in whose eyes the tear
Stood tremulous, and thus would fain have said,
If Nature had not tied her struggling tongue:
'Unkind, O! who shall now with fattening milk,
With flesh, with bread, and fish beloved, and meat,
Regale my taste? and at the cheerful fire,
Ah, who shall bask me in their downy lap?
Who shall invite me to the bed, and throw
The bedclothes o'er me in the winter night,
When Eurus roars? Beneath whose soothing hand
Soft shall I purr? But now, when Lisy's gone,

What is the dull officious world to me?
I loathe the thoughts of life.' Thus plained the cat,
While Lisy felt, by sympathetic touch,
These anxious thoughts that in her mind revolved,
And casting on her a desponding look,
She snatched her in her arms with eager grief,
And mewing, thus began: 'O Cat beloved!
Thou dear companion of my tender years!
Joy of my youth! that oft has licked my hands
With velvet tongue ne'er stained by mouse's blood.
Oh, gentle Cat! how shall I part with thee?
How dead and heavy will the moments pass
When you are not in my delighted eye,
With Cubi playing, or your flying tail.
How harshly will the softest muslim feel,
And all the silk of schools, while I no more
Have your sleek skin to soothe my softened sense?
How shall I eat while you are not beside
To share the bit? How shall I ever sleep
While I no more your lulling murmurs hear?
Yet we must part – so rigid fate decrees –
But never shall your loved idea dear
Part from my soul, and when I first can mark
The embroidered figure on the snowy lawn,
Your image shall my needle keen employ.

Hark! now I'm called away! O direful sound!
I come – I come, but first I charge you all –
You – you – and you, particularly you,
O Mary, Mary, feed her with the best,
Repose her nightly in the warmest couch,
And be a Lisy to her!' – Having said,
She set her down, and with her head across,
Rushed to the evil which she could not shun,
While a sad mew went knelling to her heart!

James Thomson (1700–1748)

Familiar

When I lie on the rug
the cat settles
in the small of my back
and we are a camel.

When I sit on the chair
in my big woolly jumper
the cat burrows under
and we're seven months gone.

When I stand by the window
longing to fly
my wings are rolled up
purring, across my shoulders.

When I'm trying to sleep
on a cold winter's night
I am near stifled
by a rumbling fur hat.

When I'm cooking our fish
and she tries to be slippers
I am a stumbling monster
she, a mouse under the dresser.

Valerie Thornton (b.1954)

The Cat's Tale

The cat doesn't understand
about reading
or the space between
my eyes and the paper
or the stillness.
The silence.

She pops up
between my propped elbows
soft as peach and ashes
under my chin
executes feline twirls
then lodges her tail
below my nose
so I can smell
how clean she is.

She sits on the page
translates the words
into thrumming
cheek⁄butts my nose
jaggy⁄licks my eyelid shut
and spins me
a compelling tale
of love beyond words.

Valerie Thornton (b.1954)

A Cat

fastidious at each step
is nimble in mischance
though fearful of descent

   a peacock in its grooming

obsessed by novelty
is unwearied in waiting
yet restless at a whim

   a serpent in its gait

feigning indifference
is desolate when thwarted
then dawdles with its prey

   an introvert in pleasure

scorning to be commanded
is servile in its begging
but gives of love unasked

   an extrovert in hate

Gael Turnbull (1928–2004)

Otis

I'd like to see you in my dreams, old cat,
nose pushing at the door
in welcome; warming your snowy
underside at the fire; ginger hovis
on my lap. Instead, I can't help
seeing you in your last minutes
staring at us with blind open eyes,
wheezing as your lungs shut down,
as all of you shut down,
your chin coming to rest
on the table as the drugs took
hold, put you to dreamless sleep.

Hamish Whyte (b.1947)

GLOSSARY

Alba, Scotland
anerly, only
ase, ashes
ava, at all
birr, energy
buk heid, hide-and-seek
burd, board, table
burges, town
campsho, crooked
cheetie, catty
clukis, claws
cooring, crouching
daffine, folly
dander, stroll, wander
dicht, wipe, wash
douce, pleasant, sober, 'nice'
Eurus, east wind
fushionless, feeble
gansell, sauce
gar, make
gie, very
gin, if
Gilmore Hill, site of
    Glasgow University
gudeman, husband
hurklin, crouching
kebuck, cheese
kenspeckle, well known
knoost, lump
louping, leaping

lug, ear
mangerie, feasting
mickle, large
mingit, mingled
mutch, woman's cap
nignyes, trifles
pale, test a cheese by incision
parraling, wall hanging
pirn, weavers' bobbin
pow, head
prive, prove, test
raiket, worked over, discussed
rottens, rats
sclent, position, angle
skaith, harm
smoored, drowned
speir, ask
suas, up with
tenting, seeing
thraw, twist, distort
thrum, loose end (of threads)
uponlandis, country
wame, stomach
Wood, Wendy (1892-1981),
    Scottish nationalist activist
worset, worsted
Young, Douglas (1913-73),
    Greek scholar and Scottish
    nationalist

NOTES ON SOURCES, ETC.

J.K. Annand, 'Cat and Mous'. From *Sing It Aince for Pleasure* (Macdonald, 1965), a book of verse for children.

Joanna Baillie, 'The Kitten'. From *Fugitive Verses* (1840). Baillie was born in Bothwell and was best known in her time for her tragedies, highly praised by Scott.

Robert Bain, 'The Cat and the Man'. From *Mice and Men* (Glasgow: John Wylie, 1941). Glasgow-born Bain was a journalist, poet and playwright and an ally of MacDiarmid's in the revival of Scots as a literary language (see his 'Scottish Poetry of Today' in *Burns Chronicle second series, 1*, 1926).

'Baudron's Sang'. Taken from *A Book of Scottish Verse*, ed. George Burnett (Methuen, 1932).

George Bruce, 'Poetry Circle in a Square Room'. From *Collected Poems* (Polygon, 2001).

Gerry Cambridge, 'Tale of a Cat'. From *Madame Fifi's Farewell* (Luath, 2003).

'Little Drama'. From *The Shell House* (Scottish Cultural Press, 1995).

'The Cameronian Cat'. From *The Jacobite Relics of Scotland*, ed. James Hogg (1819). The Cameronians were fundamentalist followers of Richard Cameron, a Scottish Covenanter, who was executed in 1680. They eventually became the Reformed Presbyterian Church of Scotland.

Kate Clanchy, 'Towards the End'. From *Slattern* (Chatto, 1995).

Stewart Conn, 'Visitation'. From *Ghosts at Cockcrow* (Bloodaxe, 2005).

Anna Crowe, 'Cat and Water'. From *Punk with Dulcimer* (Peterloo Poets, 2006).

John Cunningham, 'The Fox and the Cat'. From *Poems, Chiefly Pastoral, 2nd ed.* (Newcastle, 1771). Poet, playwright and actor, Cunningham just squeezes in, as, though Dublin-born, he was of Scottish descent.

Catherine Czerkawska, 'Apart'. From 'Two Moments', *Weekend Scotsman*, 10 January 1981.

M.L. Dalgleish, 'An Edinburgh Cat'. From *Artifex and Other Poems* (Edinburgh: C.J. Cousland & Sons, 1964).

Graham Fulton, 'Wee Plebs'. From *Photographing Ghosts* (Roncadora Press, forthcoming).

'Remainders'. From *Full Scottish Breakfast* (Red Squirrel Press, 2011).

Valerie Gillies, 'Black Cat Boy'. From *Men and Beasts* (Luath, 2000).

Isobel Gowdie of Auldearne, cat spell. From *Pitcairn's Criminal Trials III*, pp.607-8. 'home again' means back into her own shape. (See Robert Graves, *The White Goddess*, 1961 ed., pp.401-2).

W.S. Graham, 'Master Cat and Master Me'. This mysterious poem is from *New Collected Poems* (Faber, 2004).

Alexander Gray, 'On a Cat, Ageing'. From *Gossip* (Porpoise Press, 1928).

Jen Hadfield, 'In the same way'. From *Nigh-No-Place* (Bloodaxe, 2008).

Diana Hendry, 'Cat in the Apple Tree'. Previously unpublished.

Kate Hendry, 'Taking Care of Fear'. Previously unpublished.

Robert Henryson, 'Gib Hunter, our jolie Cat'. This extract is from 'The Taill of the Uponlandis Mous and the Burges Mous' in his *Morall Fabillis of Esope*, written probably in the 1470s. It has been suggested that the cat, Gib, represents James III of Scotland, who could have been thought of as playing with his subjects as the cat does with the country mouse. (See Robert L. Kindrick, 'Lion or Cat? Henryson's Characterization of James III', *Studies in Scottish Literature* vol. XIV, 1979).

Ellen Johnston, 'Nellie's Lament for the Pirnhouse Cat . . .'. From *Poems and Songs* (Glasgow, 1867). Hamilton-born Johnston had a brief period of fame as the 'Poetical Factory Girl'. She died in the Barony Poorhouse, Glasgow.

Jackie Kay, 'The Nine Lives of the Cat Mandu'. From *Red, Cherry Red* (Bloomsbury, 2007).

Archie Lamont, 'Sam and Jock the Lallans Cats'. From *Sam and Jock the Lallans Cats* (Scottish Secretariat, 1950). Lamont was a geologist and a Scottish nationalist activist.

Maurice Lindsay, 'Between Two Worlds'. From *Collected Poems 1940-1990* (Aberdeen University Press, 1990).

George MacBeth, 'Fourteen Ways of Touching the Peter'. From *The Night of Stones* (Macmillan, 1968. Reprinted in *Collected Poems 1958-1982*.

'To the Flea, Combed from my Cat's Back'. From *Prayers* (Aquila, 1973).

Brian McCabe, 'The Cat'. From *Lines Review 90*, 1984. Reprinted in *From One Atom to Another* (Polygon, 1987).

Norman MacCaig, 'Black Cat in a Morning'. From *The Poems of Norman MacCaig* (Polygon, 2005).

Dugald S. McColl, 'Connoisseurs'. From *Poems* (Blackwell, 1940). As well as a painter and art historian Glasgow-born McColl was keeper of the Tate Gallery and the Wallace Collection.

James McGonigal, 'Claire with the Hindlegs'. Previously unpublished.

Paddy McGown, 'The Old Tom Cat'. This song was sung by 'the renowned' Paddy McGown in the Shakespeare Saloon, Glasgow, in 1855. It was printed at the Poet's Box, 6 St Andrew's Lane, and sold as a penny broadsheet.

Alasdair Maclean, 'My Cat Asleep'. From *Waking the Dead* (Gollancz, 1976).

Joseph Gordon Macleod, 'A Strange Cat Got In'. From *Lines Review 20*, Summer 1963. Scotland's 'lost' modernist, he also wrote as Adam Drinan.

Gordon Meade, 'Catfish'. From *Pig Squealing* (ASLS, 1992; *New Writing Scotland 10*). Reprinted in *The Scrimshaw Sailor* (*Chapman*, 1996).

Richard Medrington, 'Bully Cat'. From *The Thing That Mattered Most: Scottish Poems for Children*, ed. Julie Johnstone (Scottish Poetry Library / Black & White Publishing, 2006).

Edwin Morgan, 'The Cat'. From *Tales from Limerick Zoo* (Mariscat Press, 1988).

'Like, Little Russian Cat'. From *Starryveldt* (Eugen Gomringer Press, 1965). 'KAK is the Russian for "like", and KOTEHOK (pronounced "katyonok") for "kitten" (diminutive of KOT = "cat"). The title also uses "like" as a sixties vogue-word. I liked the two Russian words because they didn't need any special letters in English.' (EM)

'Scotch Cat'. From *Starryveldt*.

'Three Cats'. From Ian Hamilton Finlay's magazine *Poor. Old. Tired. Horse. no. 12*, 1964.

James Munce, 'Lines on a Cat and Bird Show in Glasgow'. From *Poems*, 2nd ed. (Glasgow, 1881).

John Murray, 'The Meenister's Cat'. From *Scream, if You Want to Go Faster* (ASLS, 1991; *New Writing Scotland 9*). Architectural lecturer Murray's amusing variations on the old parlour game.

William Neill, 'Cat Accident'. From *Selected Poems 1969-1992* (Canongate, 1994).

Nursery Rhymes. From a variety of sources, notably the indispensable *Scottish Nursery Rhymes*, collected and edited by Norah and William Mongomerie (Hogarth Press, 1964). 'Pussy-cat, Pussy-cat' must be one of the best known of all nursery rhymes; the Scottish version ('Poussie, Poussie Baudrons') first appeared in print in the 1842 edition of Robert Chambers's *The Popular Rhymes of Scotland*, with the cat going to see the king and the 'guid fat mousikie' merely a 'wee mousie'. The version printed here is from the 1870 edition.

Tom Pow, *A Cat Suite*. Written specially for this book. I asked for a cat poem and got a sweet suite.

Alison Prince, 'The Wildcat'. From *The Whifflet Train* (Mariscat Press, 2003).

Alastair Reid, 'Propinquity', 'Cat-Faith' and 'Curiosity'. All from *Weathering* (Canongate, 1978). Reprinted in *Inside Out: Selected Poetry & Translations* (Polygon, 2008).

Dilys Rose, 'Nightlife'. From *Twinset* (Knucker Press, 2008).

Iain Crichton Smith, 'The Cat'. From *Images 2*, 1986.

'The Cat'. From *Collected Poems* (Carcanet, 1992).

'The Wildcat'. From *River, River* (Macdonald, 1978).

Sydney Goodsir Smith, 'Stormy Day and a Cat, November'. From *Akros 24*, April 1974.

James Thomson, 'Lisy's Parting with her Cat'. Elizabeth was the poet's favourite sister and this poem for her was written by Thomson as a boy. He later gave her money to set up as a milliner in Edinburgh. The text is from his *Poetical Works*, ed. J. Logie Robertson (Oxford University Press, 1908; Oxford Standard Authors).

Valerie Thornton, 'Familiar' and 'The Cat's Tale'. From *Catacoustics* (Mariscat Press, 1995).

Gael Turnbull, 'A Cat'. From *For Whose Delight* (Mariscat Press, 1995). Reprinted in *There Are Words: Collected Poems* (Shearsman/Mariscat, 2006).

Hamish Whyte, 'Otis'. From *A Bird in the Hand* (Shoestring Press, 2008).

BIBLIOGRAPHY

Christabel Aberconway, *A Dictionary of Cat Lovers* (Michael Joseph, 1949).

Felicity Bast, ed., *The Poetical Cat: An Anthology* (Farrar Straus Giroux, 1995).

Clare Boylan, ed., *The Literary Companion to Cats* (Sinclair-Stevenson, 1994).

Emily Fragos, ed., *The Great Cat: Poems about Cats* (Everyman's Library Pocket Poets, 2005).

George MacBeth and Martin Booth, eds, *The Book of Cats* (Martin Secker & Warburg, 1976; Bloodaxe Books, 1992).

Hamish Whyte, ed., *The Scottish Cat* (Aberdeen University Press, 1987).

ACKNOWLEDGEMENTS

For help and encouragement along the way, I'd like to thank Ian Campbell, Stewart Conn, Diana Hendry, Jim Hutcheson and Tom Johnstone (my designer and editor at Birlinn), Lizzie MacGregor of the Scottish Poetry Library and Enda Ryan of the Mitchell Library. I'd especially like to thank all the poets, poets' estates and publishers who kindly gave permission for poems to be reprinted in this book – these are detailed below. Every effort was made to trace copyright holders; where this has proved impossible and the work has been included in the anthology, it is with apologies and in the hope that such use will be welcomed. Corrections will be gratefully received.

J.K. Annand, 'Cat and Mous', reprinted by permission of Scottish Language Dictionaries; George Bruce, 'Poetry Circle in a Square Room' reprinted by permission of Polygon; Gerry Cambridge, 'Tale of a Cat' and 'Little Drama', reprinted by permission of the poet; Kate Clanchy, 'Towards the End', reprinted by permission of the poet and Picador; Stewart Conn, 'Visitation', reprinted by permission of the poet and Bloodaxe Books; Anna Crowe, 'Cat and Water', reprinted by permission of the poet; Catherine Czerkawska, 'Apart', reprinted by permission of the poet; Graham Fulton, 'Wee Plebs' and 'Remainders', reprinted by permission of the poet; Valerie Gillies, 'Black Cat Boy', reprinted by permission of the poet; W.S. Graham, 'Master Cat and Master Me', reproduced by permission of Rosalind Mudaliar, the estate of W.S. Graham; Alexander Gray, 'On a Cat, Ageing', reprinted by permission of Alison Webster; Jen Hadfield, 'In the same way', reprinted by permission of the poet and Bloodaxe Books; Diana Hendry, 'Cat in the Apple Tree', printed by permission of the poet; Kate Hendry, 'Taking Care of Fear', printed by permission of the poet; Jackie Kay, 'The Nine Lives of the Cat Mandu', reprinted by permission of the poet and Bloomsbury Publishing; George MacBeth, 'Fourteen Ways of Touching the Peter' taken from *Collected Poems 1958-1982* by George MacBeth © George MacBeth 1989 and

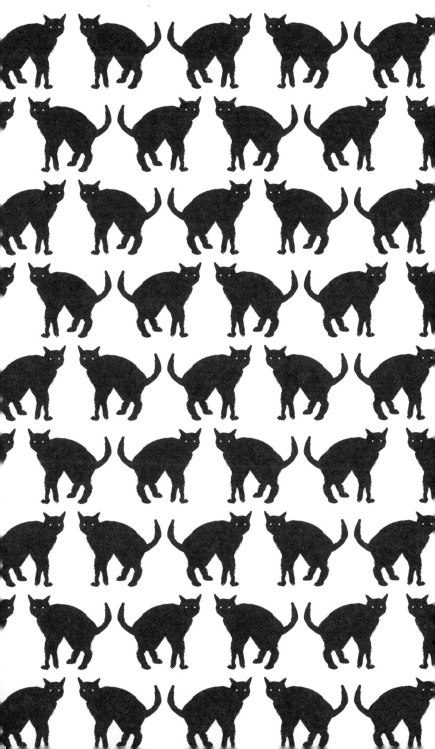

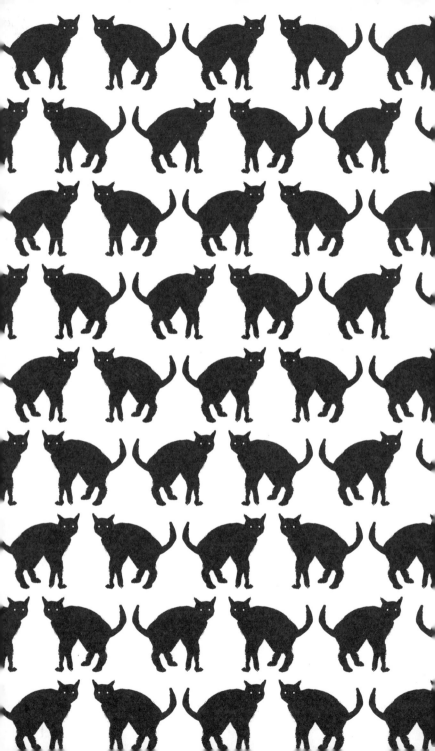